Two Naked Feet

by Maria Lisella

POETS WEAR PRADA ● HOBOKEN, NJ

Two Naked Feet

First North American Publication 2009.

Copyright © 2009 Maria Lisella

http://pwpbooks.blogspot.com/

Grateful acknowledgment is made to the following publications where some of these poems have previously appeared or will soon appear:

Feile-Festa, New York Quarterly, Pirene's Fountain, Skidrow Penthouse, and in the chapbook series, *Annual Brevitas Festival of the Short Poem*, published by First Street Press.

ISBN 978-0-9841844-1-5

Printed in the U.S.A.

Front Cover Collage: Roxanne Hoffman

Author's Photo: Stillman Rogers

Due piedi nudi
cercando il tramonto
dimenticando del tempo
nè ieri nè domani

Two naked feet
searching for the sunset
forgetting time
neither yesterday nor tomorrow

Contents

Acknowledgements

About the Author

Ladies Who Lunch

at Le Bernardin prefer oysters
no larger than two inches.
Briny, muscular, manageable,
the most popular are widow's holes,
like a punch line to a dirty joke
about the world's favorite aphrodisiac.
Instead, it is named for a widow
married to a lost-at-sea whaler
who lived on the Peconic
where oysters are born, bred,
cultivated to lady-like taste.
If left alone, can live for fifteen years,
grow to foot-long sea creatures.
Almost inert, inanimate as a plant,
oysters live sealed inside shells,
filled with their own liquor.
Take one firm bite
or the creature will live on
in your stomach, say the French.
Puff your cheek with its liquor,
taste the salty air, a sweet creature.
Slurp, never chew. Tease it,
work it with your tongue,
never sink your teeth in, goodness no.
Yet others say, *If you swallow,*
all oysters are the same.

Mantras

She went to India to memorize
To study on bended knee, head bowed
To utter ohhhhhhm
Follow her breath rise fall
through the fine cilia
that line her nostrils
departing at the count of eight
Hushed whisper travels well
from nose to mouth and back
Not unlike repeating the rosary
fingers following the chained circle
one bead at a time.

Un Beso in Cuba

Back with your right
forward with your left
Cross body turn – press her.
Let her know it's coming.
¡Ahora, enchufa!

Los Van Van swings
a *ritmo Cubano*.
Smutty studio windows
the wooden floor pale and
polished under dancing feet
sliding, stepping,
pounding, turning.
A door slips open —
Cuban couple whose feet are
loving the moment.

Let her foot get in the middle
your feet stay on the outside.
¡Ahora, una vuelta!

I look down at the pattern
un beso with his pelvis
his feet frame mine.
Can lesson one get
this sexy, this fast
in sultry Havana?

Breakfast in Baiona

Salt and pepper mane,
angular nose, an exact
reproduction of his father's.
The son's still supple spine
curves over his father's plate.

Fresh berries, melon
peeled and cut into bite-sizes.

The father's face is Goya-long,
pale, collapsed skin belies
once sharp planes,
a waist soft and round.
Arms locked at his sides.

They dine in near silence
but for the clink of fork and knife.

The father's eyes look straightforward
never meeting his son's, whose soft
voice whispers sounds in rolling Spanish
into his father's ear. They rise as one.
Son holds the father's deadened arm,

as they make their way to the bay
from which Columbus set sail for America.

Romance

I stand beneath
the Eiffel Tower's black steel netting

Knowing my father's French past
kept him one step beyond
the surly brood of Italian men
filing into the parlor on Sundays.

A WWII vet, he worked
with the Senegalese, Algerians
he tutored me
in an ethical landscape of honor,
loyalty – old-fashioned words.

He and his friends Yves, Viggo, Rolanda
never belied their resistance days
ordinary heroics in a living room in Queens.

Autumn in the Algarve

Cherry-faced
Brits, Germans
with crooked teeth,
fast smiles
bellies bouncing in buggies
over and under Algarve
golf courses
off season, half-price.
Breakfast tables
piled high with croissants,
rolls, Portuguese tortillas
under a canopy facing
the Atlantic rolling
to the sounds of Cape Verde,
dining on coffee from Angola,
shrimp from Mozambique,
pride from the north,
courtesy of Portugal's
children disguised
as butlers and maids.

Game

Clouds of steam from his nostrils.
Blood splatters with guttural grunts
on mustard sand in *el corrido*.
Spectators sit in *el sol* or *la sombra*
sipping whiskey from tidy glasses.
Stomping their feet flamenco style
for a speedy end to a sloppy kill.

Mad with Fear

She stands alone atop a bleached white
fortress overlooking the turquoise Adriatic.
The dry *bura* wind brushes
the heat of spring's sun over her skin,
a wind only nature could invent
and usually saves for winter.

Franiça moved to Dubrovnik's old city
protected by tall, thick limestone walls.
Not for a moment did we think
they would bomb the Old Town.
Not Napoleon, not Hitler did such a thing.

Even when the bombs fell in the "shelling hours,"
We slept sometimes for sixteen hours a day.
I have never slept so many hours.
So much of my life… just spent sleeping.
Sometimes when we woke
we could not hear, we could not speak.

Her pale, wide-spaced eyes
sag at the outer corners.
I wonder if they looked that way
before the war, before the shelling,
before the long sleeps,
before sharing five liters
of water each day among so many
who needed to drink or bathe.

At night we tied our wrists one to another
so we could not be lost,
her head lifts, eyes lock on mine for the first time.
And we laughed for no reason. Mad with fear.

Sparrow Hawks

They call us sparrow hawks,
the smallest birds of prey
at ten inches. They prefer open spaces.
The human variety deviates.
Works instead in crowded urban centers,
finds solace in anonymity yet remain
visible as hostesses or stewardesses
in hotels, on ships, airplanes.

These falcon family birds hover
above intended prey,
which is smaller still
birds, spiders, reptiles, grasshoppers,
crickets, mice, caterpillars.

Western women pity us, our
men scorn us, and our sisters
fear for us, the veil, illiteracy,
genital mutilation, we seem
hopeless, backward, astray.

Men call them
sparrow hawks of neocolonialism,
women who have unnaturally
used their energies for materialism,
instead of as "god" intended.

La Nebbia Veneziana (Fog in Venice)

Robed and twice-twined
with the plush terry cloth robe
that came with my posh room,
I dress for the steaming pool
on this chilly winter night.

The first night of *Carnevale* in Venice
beyond this mineral bath
children run among the shadows
with red capes, devils' horns,
men wear three-cornered hats
as they do in *Rigoletto*
and women press bulbous breasts
above lace bodices and jeweled skirts.

I can barely see the pool
the fog is so thick
the steam heady — the odor
of boiled eggs rising.

The fog never touches me,
never settles on any surface
swift as a breath,
steam without the fear of heat,
a mist that leaves shadows in the spotlight.

I part the steam with each movement.
It folds over me, behind me,
protects me from the cold night air,

from the light, from the eyes
of the other solitary swimmer.

I hear the water
part in lopsided movements.
Not synchronized,
but in jagged intervals.
He is passing me.
He is invisible.

I would like to ask him to swim in silence,
to make no waves in this temple of steam.

Abruzzo in Spring

Like a Buddha, a man sits squarely
facing the Adriatic
train tracks behind him as he waits
for the sea to *riscaldera*
warm itself up again,
to the strains of a Brazilian beat.

Tattooed *gelati* lickers
boys with *telefoninis* stuck
to their ears, heads wrapped
in sunglasses. *Le donne* in
suits and sandals.

Men on *vespas lungomare*,
along the water,
babies in their laps
flowers tucked in their saddles.

Zone

The eyes and ears have it
the nose, too.
She shadows people's sounds
in bars, restaurants,
charts their courses
across crowded rooms.

Peopled subway cars, a mine
of foreign bodies violating
the 18-inch comfort zone,
flesh pressed against flesh,
against steel, poles protect.
Conversations spoken nose-to-nose
erupt and simmer.

She sneaks up behind them —
a Mata Hari of the spoken word
non-sequitirs seep into her pen,
appear on her pages
compel her to scribble,
stealing strangers' whispers

she revisits her notebooks
to discover a germ,
a word that sings or rises or claps
or makes a striking sound,
leaping off the pad in surprise or ecstasy.

So many trail like mouse droppings
leading nowhere; to be swept away
in favor of more perfect moments
that may one day
sit cross-legged on a tightrope
like smiling acrobats in the sun.

Acknowledgements

"Ladies Who Lunch" appeared in *The New York Quarterly*, Number 64, 2008.

"*Un Beso* in Cuba" was one of a suite of poems that won in the semi-finalist category for the *Paumanok Poetry Award 2007*.

"Romance," "Game" and "Abruzzo in Spring" have appeared in the chapbook series, *Annual Brevitas Festival of the Short Poem*, published by First Street Press, 2008.

"*La Nebbia Veneziana* (Fog in Venice)" has appeared in *Skidrow Penthouse*, 2006; and will appear online on *Pirene's Fountain* in Fall, 2009 and in *Feile-Festa* in 2010.

About the Author

Maria Lisella is the Program Coordinator for the Italian American Writers Association readings at the Cornelia St. Café, and is co-editing an anthology based on those readings. She lives in Long Island City and was a finalist in the competition for Poet Laureate of Queens in 2007. A longtime travel writer, she currently edits a national travel trade magazine and is a member of the New York Travel Writers Association.

Her travel writing has appeared in many publications such as *Alta Cucina* (online), *Diversion, Elite Traveler, Global Foodie, Incentive Magazine, Travel & Leisure, The Boston Herald, Fra Noi, German Life, The New York Daily News, Newark Star Ledger,* and the Dubai-based *Destinations of the World.* She has spelunked in caves in Madhya Pradesh, white water rafted the Jordan River, zip-lined with monkeys in Costa Rica, ridden horseback in the foothills of Mt. Kilimanjaro, soared over the Masai Mara in a hot-air balloon, snorkeled in the Great Barrier Reef, sipped Armagnac in Gascony, and hiked Mt. Etna in Sicily.

Lisella is a member of the online poetry circle, *Brevitas,* now in its sixth year of producing the Annual *Brevitas* Festival of the Short Poem at the Bowery Poetry Club. Her writing has earned her Honorable Mention in the Allen Ginsburg Poetry Award in 2007 and in 2008, as well as from the Canadian Italian Writers Association, and for the Paolucci Award for Italian American Writing in 2003. A short story received 2nd prize from Chusma House and another will appear in the forthcoming anthology, *More Sweet Lemons, Writing with a Sicilian Accent.*